The Gaslighting Guide For Women:

DISCOVER HOW TO RECOGNIZE NARCISSISTS, BREAK FREE FROM MANIPULATION AND BUILD HEALTHY RELATIONSHIPS AFTER ABUSE

GEORGIA RAY

© Copyright 2022 Meyer House Press - All rights reserved.

The content contained within this book may not be reproduced, duplicated or transmitted without direct written permission from the author or the publisher.

Under no circumstances will any blame or legal responsibility be held against the publisher, or author, for any damages, reparation, or monetary loss due to the information contained within this book, either directly or indirectly.

Legal Notice:

This book is copyright protected. It is only for personal use. You cannot amend, distribute, sell, use, quote or paraphrase any part, or the content within this book, without the consent of the author or publisher.

Disclaimer Notice:

Please note the information contained within this document is for educational and entertainment purposes only. All effort has been executed to present accurate, up to date, reliable, complete information. No warranties of any kind are declared or implied. Readers acknowledge that the author is not engaged in the rendering of legal, financial, medical or professional advice. The content within this book has been derived from various sources. Please consult a licensed professional before attempting any techniques outlined in this book.

By reading this document, the reader agrees that under no circumstances is the author responsible for any losses, direct or indirect, that are incurred as a result of the use of the information contained within this document, including, but not limited to, errors, omissions, or inaccuracies.

Contents

Preface	9
Introduction	13

1. THE NARCISSIST'S PLAYBOOK — 19
What is a narcissist, exactly?	18
HOW TO RECOGNIZE A NARCISSIST	20
Expectations	22
Exaggeration and lies	24
Manipulation	25
Thin-Skinned Narcissist	26
What Motivates a Narcissist?	27
Chapter Summary	28

2. WHAT IS GASLIGHTING? — 31
SYMPTOMS OF GASLIGHTING ABUSE... And Why They Matter	31
COPE WITH GASLIGHTING BY LEARNING TO RECOGNIZE THE METHODS USED	34
HOW TO PROTECT YOURSELF WHEN DEALING WITH A GASLIGHTER	35
Chapter Summary	37

3. THE STAGES OF GASLIGHTING — 41
1. The Charm Offensive	41
2. The Devaluation Phase	42
3. The Discard Phase	43
Chapter Summary	45

4. GASLIGHTING IN OTHER RELATIONSHIPS ... 49
   Parents or Caregivers ... 49
   Friends ... 49
   Coworkers or Bosses ... 50
   Romantic Partners ... 50
   Gaslighting from Strangers ... 51
   Summary ... 52

5. THE IMPACT OF GASLIGHTING ... 59
   Disbelief and confusion ... 59
   Defense Mechanisms ... 60
   Depression ... 61
   Addiction ... 61
   Out of Control ... 62
   Tired all the time ... 63
   Victimized ... 63
   Short-Term Effects of Gaslighting ... 64
   Long Term Effects of Gaslighting ... 65
   What Should I Do? ... 65
   What will happen if I stay? ... 66
   Chapter Summary ... 67

6. HOW TO FIGHT BACK ... 71
   Stand Up for Yourself ... 71
   Balance Your Emotional State ... 73
   In Case You Can't Leave. ... 74
   Facing Your Gaslighter ... 75
   How to Leave an Abusive Relationship ... 77
   Tips for Dealing with Gaslighters ... 78
   Conclusion ... 78
   Chapter Summary ... 79

7. RECOVERING FROM ABUSE AND NARCISSISM ... 83
- Victim or Victorious? ... 84
- Educate Yourself ... 84
- Love Yourself ... 84
- Let Go of Closure ... 86
- Forget Shame, Guilt, and Responsibility ... 87
- Meditate and Spend Time Alone...Seriously! ... 87
- Rebuild Yourself ... 89
- Reconnect with Your Higher Self ... 89
- The Art of Volunteering ... 90
- Give Yourself Credit...For Everything That You Do Well! ... 90
- Listen To Your Body's Wisdom ... 91
- Grieve The Losses ... 92
- Allow Yourself To Feel The Emotions Fully ... 92
- Accept What Happened And Who You Are Today! ... 93
- Create New Relationships ... 93
- Give It Time ... 94
- You Are Not Alone ... 94
- Chapter Summary ... 95

Final Words ... 97
Acknowledgments ... 99
About the Author ... 101
References ... 103

Dedication

To every woman whose been scorned by a narcissist or has been gaslighted into loving a man who pretended to love her.

You deserve better and you will find better. I believe in you! <3

Preface

Narcissistic behavior doesn't come out of nowhere . It's not like this guy just decided to act evil one day. He probably had some narcissistic traits throughout childhood, but outright narcissism often develops in adulthood due to abuse/trauma, certain psychological processes (like gaslighting or thought suppression), defense mechanisms that prevent therapists from recognizing what's actually going on, and increasing levels of entitlement that are reinforced by society.

"When you're a little kid it can feel really scary if your parents aren't having a good day," Ray says. "You have no control over these big emotions they experience." That vulnerability makes kids into excellent targets for predators because they're the most easily controlled. "They're like these little soldiers that are just primed to please somebody else."

In adulthood, this process often happens in romantic relationships. Narcissists test their targets for vulnerability with a slow buildup of love-bombing and gaslighting. They shower you with attention and flattery, picking out things about yourself that you're insecure about and making them sound magical or special. You feel seen by someone who's powerful, interesting, talented — basically everything you wish you were.

You give those impossible standards a shot because maybe if you try hard enough, it can work out . But as soon as something doesn't go perfectly according to their plan (i.e., as soon as you stop putting your needs on the backburner), narcissists pull out their most powerful weapon: gaslighting.

"Gaslighting is a form of emotional abuse where somebody tries to convince you that you're crazy, making up events or feelings that never happened," Ray says. "They might say something like, 'I could have sworn I told you that' or 'That was just a misunderstanding.' Gaslighters are constantly rewriting history because they're so afraid of being exposed."

You can't trust yourself to accurately represent reality when your abuser invalidates your thoughts and emotions. You start to blame yourself for things not working out under the logic that you couldn't possibly be good enough for them. But here's the thing: It wasn't ever about you.

The gaslighter is the boss in this relationship, and if they say it didn't happen that way, then by definition it didn't. Your version of events might be logical, but their emotions are more important than yours. If you try to argue back, they're likely to play the victim or turn things around on you. They take away your ability to make decisions because now it's all about them.

If you were following along up to this point thinking "this sounds like my ex-boyfriend," congratulations! You could be dealing with a narcissist. But wait—it gets worse. The next part of Ray's book dives into how these processes develop in childhood and throughout for people who don't have narcissistic personality disorder (NPD), but who engage in similar manipulative behaviors.

"You're looking at people who have a lot of the traits of narcissism, but don't meet all the diagnostic criteria for the disorder," Ray says. "These are people who might be really good at hiding what's going on or might only engage in these behaviors some of the time."

Many of us have been in relationships with someone like this at one point or another. They can be really hard to spot because they often come across as really nice and understanding. They make you feel like you're the only person in the world they care about. But underneath that mask, they're just waiting for their next opportunity to manipulate you into doing what they want.

If you're in a relationship with someone who makes you feel crazy, misunderstood, and alone, it's time to get out. You deserve to be with someone who loves and respects you, not someone who takes advantage of your vulnerability. Seek out help from a therapist or support group so that you can start to rebuild your self-esteem and learn how to trust yourself again.

It can be really hard to leave an abusive relationship, but you're not alone. There are people who care about you and want to help. You can do this.

Introduction

You've been feeling a little off lately. You're not sure what it is, but you keep having this nagging, unsettled feeling that your partner is doing something behind your back, and you can't quite put your finger on it. It's hard to describe, but it's like nothing you know of. But the more time goes on, the more intense this feeling becomes, and the harder you try to make sense of things, the worse it feels. So what does all this mean?

It could be that someone has started gaslighting you!

This book will teach you how to identify potential narcissists, understand their motives and learn why they go about the way they do. It will also teach you what well-meaning people might have been doing wrong so far, as well as show you specific ways of telling whether someone is gaslighting you or not.

WHAT IS GASLIGHTING?

Gaslighting is a form of psychological manipulation that aims to make the victim question his or her own sanity by distorting facts, information, thoughts, feelings, and memories until he/she believes that reality isn't what it used to be. This makes the victim completely dependent on his or her abuser and often causes the latter's identity to change in order to reflect their abuser's perceptions of them.

Gaslighting generally starts off very subtly such that the gaslighter can deny any wrongdoing when confronted. However, once you've noticed that something is up, it becomes much harder for your abuser to deny due to the sheer volume of evidence against them. This is where they resort to blaming you for everything and claiming that they never meant the things they said in the first place (but you know better). To add insult to injury, once you begin questioning all their manipulative actions and statements, he/she will coax you back into believing in him by making small gestures of kindness and love towards you, which make you wonder whether all this was really worth your time.

INTRODUCTION

There are many other destructive patterns that gaslighters employ to keep their victims at bay, but these aren't as important as recognizing the effects of being a victim of gaslighting. Such effects may include:

- Subconsciously losing track of dates, times, and events in your life.
- Feeling confused about who or what caused a particular issue.
- Distancing yourself from friends and family because you feel guilty about constantly needing them to reaffirm their support for you
- Feeling down most of the time
- Having nightmares or intrusive thoughts about past interactions with your abuser
- Questioning why you have been so unhappy lately even though nothing has changed since before your relationship
- Troubling memories resurfacing without reason
- Being unable to sleep due to having nightmares or reliving memories in your mind

I will discuss these in detail in subsequent chapters. For now, let's just say that recognizing the signs of gaslighting is very important if you want to prevent further damage.

INTRODUCTION

WHAT YOU WILL LEARN FROM THIS BOOK

Through this book, you will learn:

- How narcissists generally act and how they perceive the world around them What their motives are for manipulating others
- Why you might have found yourself with one
- The effects of being manipulated by a narcissist
- How manipulators operate
- Their relationship patterns
- How long it takes before they start mistreating you
- Why victims behave in ways that drive many people up the wall (and how it can be avoided)
- Where healthy relationships end and toxic ones begin
- How you can tell if a person is a narcissist or not
- How to get help and protect yourself from further abuse
- What mental illnesses have to do with being a victim of gaslighting
- How you can regain control over your life, minimize the amount of time spent on healing and move on with your life.

INTRODUCTION

Whether you've been through anything similar before or not, the lessons in this book will give you enough insight into what went wrong in your relationship so that you can better prevent it from happening again in the future. Being able to identify narcissistic tendencies early on will allow you to steer clear of people who don't really care about your happiness and well-being. You'll come out stronger, wiser, and more confident than ever before.

The Narcissist's Playbook

Let's start with the basics:

WHAT IS A NARCISSIST, EXACTLY?

A narcissist is a person who has an excessive sense of self-importance and requires admiration from others. This sense of importance is so strong that they have difficulty sharing the spotlight with anyone, even those closest to them.

In order for your narcissist to maintain their "high," they require some form of praise, which can take the form of favors, money, or attention - even if it's just a simple text message saying "hello." If you're getting too many demands from your narcissistic partner and not enough, thank you's--you may be a victim of gaslighting.

Narcissism occurs on a spectrum - a range of narcissism, from what's considered "normal" to pathological. A narcissist rarely gets professional help due to the risk of exposure and the fact they're unaware that their personality traits are disruptive.

Narcissistic personality disorder (NPD) doesn't usually present itself until early adulthood, and it causes damage in all aspects of an individual's life: emotionally, physically, and even financially.

Example: If you've ever been married to a narcissist - you've likely wondered why your partner can be so cold and contemptuous towards you one day but then sweet-talking like everything is okay the next. It may make you worry about your mental health or think it's "all in your head." But rest assured - it's not.

Narcissists are known for their deficits in empathy, but this empathy can be "turned on" when they feel threatened by someone else's success or something that will threaten the ego. They usually do this with passive-aggressive behavior, leaving you feeling confused and hurt. This type of manipulation is called gaslighting - a particular form of mental abuse that makes victims question their own feelings, instincts, and sanity, which gives more power to the narcissist.

It's no surprise that narcissists make terrible romantic partners - they downplay your emotions while exaggerating their own, ignore problems until they escalate into full-blown attacks, prioritize themselves above others, are quick to anger if challenged or criticized, have an inability to take responsibility for themselves, and their "love" usually depends on how willing you are to give them what they want.

When a narcissist doesn't receive the attention they feel entitled to - they either withdraw or explode in anger until they can use guilt-tripping and self-pitying behavior to elicit some sympathy from you. A frequent statement of an upset narcissist is, "you don't care about me!" The more a narcissistic partner says this, the more it exacerbates your fear that there's something wrong with YOU if you don't feel empathy towards your partner. Narcissists make great actors who know how to fake emotion when it suits them.

You may think your relationship is good, but eventually, you realize everything revolved around the narcissist and their needs.

HOW TO RECOGNIZE A NARCISSIST

There are several red flags to look out for when trying to spot a narcissist:

- They have an inflated sense of self-importance and need constant admiration from others
- They lack empathy and are quick to anger or feel hurt if they're not given the attention they feel entitled to
- They take advantage of others, are often aggressive and manipulative, and have a history of failed relationships
- Everything is about them - they downplay your emotions while exaggerating their own, place themselves above others, and have difficulty taking responsibility for their actions

If you see several of these signs in someone you know, it's best to cut ties with them. Don't waste your time trying to get them to see how their actions are harmful or change their behavior.

The most important thing for you to know is that you're not alone. People who have been manipulated by a narcissist often suffer in silence because they feel embarrassed, gaslight themselves into thinking it's somehow THEIR fault, and get confused when the person who says they love them doesn't act like it.

EXPECTATIONS

If you have ever been in a relationship with someone who is narcissistic, then you know the drill all too well. A relationship with a narcissist can be really confusing and painful. You may find yourself constantly second-guessing yourself and your sanity. You may also find yourself tripping over your own feet as you try to figure out what this person wants from you. In addition, it is not at all uncommon for people in a relationship with narcissists to suffer from post-traumatic stress disorder (PTSD).

A great deal of confusion and anxiety comes from the fact that a narcissist will say one thing one day and then deny ever saying it or claim they said something else entirely. You may feel as if there are no limits on this person's ability to lie and twist facts around. And if you confront them about these things, they will often become outraged and blame YOU for their actions. Confused? Don't worry - you're only human if you feel like the rug has been pulled out from under you.

The following are some common expectations that people who have been in a relationship with a narcissist may be experiencing:

Expectation: The narcissist will show remorse and change their behavior.

Reality: After getting caught, the narcissist may claim they don't know what came over them or that it will never happen again. You can expect more apologies in the future, but these statements are simply part of the cycle because the truth is that this pattern of abuse is typical for a narcissistic person. They know how to win over people by acting sorry, but if they were truly sorry, then why not make changes? If you are waiting for contrition or true change, you are going to be waiting forever!

***

Expectation: The narcissist will be loving, attentive, and caring when they want something from me.

Reality: When the narcissist wants something from you, they can put on a great show of being loving and attentive. However, as soon as they have what they want, their attention quickly dissipates, and they move on to their next target. This is known as love-bombing, and it's a way for the narcissist to hook you in by making you feel special.

***

Expectation: I will be able to fix the narcissist

Reality: A common belief that many people who are in relationships with narcissists have is that if only they try hard enough or give enough, the narcissist will eventually change. This is not only impossible, but it's also dangerous because it can keep you in a cycle of abuse. If you are trying to fix someone who is not willing to be fixed, then you are only setting yourself up for heartbreak.

***

Expectation: The narcissist loves me

Reality: A narcissist loves themselves first and foremost. They may claim to love you, but their actions will never reflect that. In fact, a narcissist will often discard people when they are no longer useful to them, or they have outlived their usefulness.

***

EXAGGERATION AND LIES

As mentioned earlier, a narcissist is an expert at exaggeration and lying. They will often twist the truth to make themselves look better or to make you look bad. They may also lie about their past or who they are as a person. If you challenge them on any of these things, they will become defensive and attack you.

A relationship with a narcissist is often associated with extreme emotional and psychological abuse. This type of abuse includes lying, withholding or distracting you from seeing the truth, gaslighting, triangulation, and so on. If you are experiencing any of these things within your relationship, there is no way that you can trust this person because they have proven over and over again that they cannot be trusted.

MANIPULATION

Manipulation is a key tactic that narcissists use in order to get what they want. They may use guilt, coercion, or threats to control you and make you do things that you don't want to do. They may also use sympathy and flattery to make you feel sorry for them or to get you to do something for them. If you fall for any of these tactics, the narcissist will only become more manipulative in order to keep you under their thumb.

The best way to deal with manipulation is to simply not engage with it. Don't try to reason with the narcissist or try to get them to see your point of view. This will only lead to frustration and anger on your part. Simply put, don't engage with them and let them manipulate you - and remember that they are not entitled to your time, energy, or emotions.

If you are in a relationship with a narcissist, it's important to understand that things will never change. The narcissist will never truly love you, and they will never be sorry for the way that they have treated you. The best thing that you can do is to end the relationship and move on. Don't look back because the narcissist will only bring pain and heartache into your life.

THIN-SKINNED NARCISSIST

Most narcissists tend to be particularly thin-skinned. This is probably because they have a deep-seated need for constant praise and attention. They create compliments and reassurance. If a compliment is going to make them angry, then don't bother giving it to them. Remember that a compliment should never be something that comes out of obligation but rather something that comes from the heart.

If a narcissist truly loves themselves, then they would not get so angry when someone gives them a compliment or tries to flatter them in some way. The truth is that they are very easily offended by positive things and will lash out at anyone who doesn't give enough praise or flattery to keep their ego satisfied.

If you are in a relationship with someone who is thin-skinned, it's best to not give too many compliments to them as they may actually take them the wrong way. They will only feel criticized if you say something that isn't positive or that doesn't make them look good.

You may want to think twice before complimenting someone who has narcissistic tendencies because they are very likely to turn on you if your words don't flatter them enough. This is because their ego depends upon getting constant praise and recognition from others in order to survive.

WHAT MOTIVATES A NARCISSIST?

Many people wonder what motivates a narcissist. The answer is actually quite simple - they are motivated by attention and power. They want to be in control of everything and everyone around them. They also crave admiration and respect from others. If you can't give them the attention that they want or if you don't respect them, they will often lash out in anger or frustration.

Narcissists are also known to be very competitive, and they will do whatever it takes to come out on top. This may include cheating, lying, or stealing in order to get what they want. They often have a sense of entitlement which allows them to do whatever they please without any regard for other people's feelings.

CHAPTER SUMMARY

In order to recognize a narcissist, it is important to understand what motivates them. Narcissists are motivated by attention and power. They want to be in control of everything and everyone around them. They also crave admiration and respect from others. If you can't give them the attention that they want or if you don't respect them, they will often lash out in anger or frustration. Narcissists are also known to be very competitive, and they will do whatever it takes to come out on top. This may include cheating, lying, or stealing in order to get what they want. They often have a sense of entitlement which allows them to do whatever they please without any regard for other people's feelings.

What Is Gaslighting?

So...What Is Gaslighting?

Gaslighting is extremely manipulative behavior used by narcissists, sociopaths, borderline personalities, and anyone else who's intent on getting their way while hurting other people in the process. It often starts off subtly but can become incredibly destructive given enough time. If you recognize outbreaks of gaslighting in your relationship, it's important to address them immediately so your partner can't continue using this toxic tool against you!

Let's find out more about what makes gaslighting different from other types of manipulation...

- Manipulation tactics are usually used for one purpose only: to make a person do something they wouldn't want to do otherwise or give up something they dearly value.
- Gaslighting is done slowly, gradually, and with much more subtlety than other forms of manipulation. It can even be so subtle that you don't notice anything is wrong until months or years have gone by. This makes it easy for your abuser to convince you that their behavior is normal, thus allowing them to continue their toxic ways without interference.
- Its goals are to instill fear, self-doubt, and insecurity into the victim while giving them false information that supports the abuser's point of view. Gaslighters want to control both your mind and actions, leaving little room for an accurate picture of reality. The longer you're involved with someone who gaslight the, less able you are to trust your own instincts.

SYMPTOMS OF GASLIGHTING ABUSE... AND WHY THEY MATTER

Signs That You're A Victim of Gaslighting

Before you can stop an abuser, it's important to understand what makes this type of person tick so you can comprehend what they're doing and why. Understanding the driving force behind gaslighting is critical if you want to stop the pain but let's briefly pinpoint some warning signs first:

There are several reasons narcissists employ gaslighting tactics, but their goals are always the same:

1. To gain control over another person
2. To hide something embarrassing or incriminating
3. To avoid being exposed or held accountable for their actions
4. To get their way

When it comes to relationships, gaslighting can take many forms. Some of the most common and recognizable ones include:

- **Blocking and diverting:** this is when your abuser pretends they haven't heard you or says something contrary to what you actually said to make you doubt yourself.
- **Denial:** this usually comes in the form of outright denying things they've said or done which are documented proof otherwise. It can also happen with more complex behaviors too,

like saying hurtful things yet expecting full forgiveness because 'they're sorry'
- **Countering:** happens when your abuser questions your memory about specific events in order to make you question yourself. This one works hand in hand with denial, where if you deny something enough times, people will start to believe it's normal while discounting any memories that prove otherwise.
- **False accusations:** when your abuser turns the tables on you by accusing you of doing or saying something similar to what they're doing themselves. This makes them appear both innocent and truthful at the same time!
- **Positive refocusing:** occurs when your partner tries to divert attention away from their bad actions or behavior by trying to make you feel good about yourself in comparison. This one is the most difficult for people with low self-esteem because it encourages them to see their abuse as 'normal' while maintaining an idealized image of someone else who's worse than them (and thus deserves more mistreatment).
- **Discounting:** takes place when your abuser doesn't believe or pays no attention to what you're saying, thus subjectively discounting it. This is a favorite tactic of narcissists because it

makes them appear both innocent and truthful in one swoop!

Gaslighting can be a traumatic experience that may affect people in different ways. Some common effects include anxiety, depression, low self-esteem, anger, lowered sex drive, and much more... But don't despair - there's always hope when you find the right tools for healing your mind from trauma. I suggest checking out this free resource list to get started with learning how to recognize abuse tactics and protect yourself from further mistreatment.

COPE WITH GASLIGHTING BY LEARNING TO RECOGNIZE THE METHODS USED

One of the best ways to cope with a person who's gaslighting you is to learn how their mind works. Abusers have practiced using these tactics for so long it comes as second nature to them without having any emotional attachment whatsoever. They're simply tools used to make people doubt themselves and take control over their rational thoughts!

In order to stop the abuse from continuing, you first need to know what makes your abuser tick - become familiar with their mindset and try predicting their next move. This will be harder than it sounds, but if you ever want things to change, you'll need a clear head that can think objectively about everything they do or say.

Take some time out for yourself to mentally prepare yourself for what's about to come. As hard as it is, you need to be 100% confident that you will follow through with everything in order to get your abuser off your back once and for all. Let them know that you're just not going to put up with the gaslighting anymore!

HOW TO PROTECT YOURSELF WHEN DEALING WITH A GASLIGHTER

There are several ways in which people choose to cope with an abusive person. Some of these behaviors may include doing nothing, telling them 'No,' or always giving in when they make unreasonable demands. Although these methods might seem like good ideas when dealing with someone who's constantly on the offensive, many times, they end up making things worse!

STOP GIVING IN TO THEIR DEMANDS

As much as abusers love to make everything about themselves, you shouldn't cave into their demands no matter how much pressure they put on you. Abusers are used to getting what they want because people have allowed them to get away with mistreatment for so long. Instead of being passive about the situation, why not try taking a stand against it? Do whatever you can to show your abuser that their behavior won't be tolerated anymore! This will likely lead to arguments, but that's fine - it just means that you're making progress by sticking up for yourself!

SAY 'NO' TO THEIR BEHAVIOR

Instead of always giving in when your abuser badgers you, try saying 'No'. This will take a lot of strength in the beginning because chances are, they won't take no for an answer. However, if you continue to repeat this as a response, they'll eventually get the hint and move on. It may be hard in the early stages, but it's definitely worth it to see your abuser walk away frustrated!

TRY DISTANCE AS A WAY OF PROTECTION

Not everyone is comfortable standing up to their abuser face-to-face, so distance can be a great way to protect yourself. This can be done by avoiding them as much as possible or creating physical boundaries (like not allowing them into your personal space). If you're not able to do either of those things, try communicating with them through text or email instead of in person. This will give you time to properly form your thoughts before saying anything and make it less likely for them to interrupt you.

USE A SUPPORT SYSTEM

It's important to have someone to talk to who understands what you're going through. This can be a friend, family member, or therapist - just somebody who will listen and not judge. Dealing with an abuser can be very isolating, so it's crucial that you have people in your life who will help you get through this tough time.

If you or someone you know is being gaslighted, please reach out for help! You don't have to go through this alone.

CHAPTER SUMMARY

Gaslighting is a form of abuse that causes the victim to doubt their own thoughts, memories, and sanity. Abusers use gaslighting as a way to manipulate and control their victims. In order to protect themselves, victims of gaslighting need to be aware of what makes their abuser tick and learn how to predict their next move. They also need to be confident in following through with their decisions and not give in to the abuser's demands. Finally, they should reach out for help from a support system.

The Stages of Gaslighting

Gaslighting can be broken down into 3 distinct stages:

1. **The Charm Offensive** - this is when the narcissist puts on their best behavior in order to trick you into thinking he or she is the best match for you. They try to make themselves look like Prince (or Princess) Charming, who just has to love you in order to fulfill your dreams;
2. **The Devaluation Phase** - this is when the narcissist starts to put you down, making you feel like you're not good enough for them. They may say that you're too needy, too sensitive, too emotional, or that there's something wrong with you;

3. **The Discard Phase** - this is when the narcissist finally decides they've had enough of you and dumps you. They may make up excuses for why they're leaving, such as "I'm just not ready for a relationship right now," or "You deserve someone better than me."

We'll delve into each stage with an example from one of my close friends Janice who has very kindly agreed to share her experience with others so that they might avoid the same problems.

1. THE CHARM OFFENSIVE

I remember the first time I met Marcus. He was charming, outgoing, and had a roguish smile that made me feel like I was the only woman in the world. We hit it off instantly, and he swept me off my feet with his romantic gestures and declarations of love.

It didn't take long for me to realize that something was wrong - Marcus would fly into fits of rage over the smallest things and would often make hurtful comments about my appearance or intelligence. But by that point, I was already too invested in the relationship to leave. I told myself that things would get better, that Marcus loved me and just had a bad temper.

Later on, I realized that his bad temper was actually rage - he would explode over the slightest things but then would refuse to talk about it or apologize for his behavior. He would tell me that "we all have anger issues" and convince me that these fits of rage were somehow my fault.

I started to realize that something wasn't right when Marcus refused to validate any of my feelings. If I expressed concern over his explosive temper, he would tell me that I was being overly sensitive or too needy. When I tried to express my dissatisfaction with our sex life, he told me there was something wrong with me because I didn't enjoy having sex with him.

Marcus was gaslighting me, and I didn't even realize it. He was manipulating me into thinking that my feelings were wrong, that I was the one with the problem. He made me feel like I was going crazy, and I was so invested in the relationship that I couldn't see past his charm offensive.

2. THE DEVALUATION PHASE

The devaluation phase is where the narcissist starts to put you down, making you feel like you're not good enough for them. They may say that you're too needy, too sensitive, too emotional, or that there's something wrong with you.

I remember one time when Marcus told me that I was "crazy" because I got upset after he ignored me for several days. He would call me names and make fun of me in front of his friends, which made me feel like I was worthless.

The devaluation phase is also when the narcissist starts to withdraw their love and support. They may stop complimenting you or doing things that make you happy. They may start to ignore your needs and only focus on their own.

3. THE DISCARD PHASE

The discard phase is when the narcissist finally decides they've had enough of you and dumps you. They may make up excuses for why they're leaving, such as "I'm just not ready for a relationship right now," or "You deserve someone better than me."

I remember one when Marcus told me he was breaking up with me. He said that he still loved me, but he just wasn't ready for a relationship. He also told me that I was too good for him and that I deserved someone who could treat me better.

The discard phase can be incredibly painful, especially if you've been in the relationship for a long time. You may feel like you did something wrong or like you're not good enough for anyone else. You may feel like you'll never find someone else who will love you.

If you're experiencing any of these signs, it's important to realize that you're being gaslighted. This means that your partner is manipulating you into thinking that your feelings are wrong and that you're the one with the problem. If you feel like you can't get out of the relationship on your own, it's time to seek support from a mental health professional.

In today's world, many abusers are using their smartphones to intimidate and stalk their victims. This new technology has made it extremely difficult for victims of abuse to escape their perpetrators' reach. In fact, some individuals have had to hire private investigators in order to find out where their abusers are keeping them. Unfortunately, even with the help of these experts, it can be nearly impossible to track an individual who uses this tactic because they're constantly changing locations.

The best course of action is prevention. Make sure that you never leave your smartphone unattended or unlocked if you live with someone who could pose a risk to your safety. If you're in a relationship with a narcissist, it's important to keep your distance and protect yourself emotionally.

If you're being stalked or harassed by someone, it's important to contact the police and seek help from a domestic violence shelter. Remember that you're not alone, and there are people who can help you get through this difficult time.

CHAPTER SUMMARY

Gaslighting is a form of emotional abuse where you are manipulated into believing that your feelings are wrong. Gaslighters make you feel crazy and make comments about who you are to make you feel bad. They also withdraw love and support, which can make you feel like you're worthless and unlovable. If these signs sound familiar, it's important to seek help from a mental health professional. The best way to avoid gaslighting is to keep your distance from the person and to not leave your phone unattended when in their presence. If you feel like your life may be in danger or if someone is stalking or harassing you, contact the police and get help from a domestic violence shelter. Remember that there are people who can help and that you are not alone.

Gaslighting In Other Relationships

Gaslighting can occur in any type of relationship, whether it be with a partner, friend, family member, or coworker. Narcissists will use gaslighting to control and manipulate their victims in any situation that can benefit them.

Manipulative people, in general, are very good at turning things around on their victims. They will make you feel like you are the one who is crazy or wrong, even when you know you are not. This is another way of gaining control over you.

If you find someone in your life who tends to do this, be aware of their behavior and don't let them gaslight you. Stand up for yourself and maintain your own sense of reality. Don't let them make you doubt yourself.

PARENTS OR CAREGIVERS

Some parents or caregivers may gaslight their children in order to get them to do what they want. They may make the child feel like they are wrong for feeling a certain way or for wanting something. The parent may then use this guilt to control the child's behavior.

This can be very damaging to a child's development and can cause them to have low self-esteem and trust issues. It is important for the child to have a healthy relationship with at least one caregiver who will build them up and validate their feelings, not tear them down.

If you are a victim of gaslighting by a parent or caregiver, it is important to seek professional help. You may also want to consider reaching out to a support group for survivors of childhood abuse.

FRIENDS

Friends can also be guilty of gaslighting. They may make you feel like you are being too sensitive or that you are overreacting to a situation. They may try to make you doubt your own judgment and make you believe that they are always right.

This can be very damaging to a friendship, as it can cause mistrust and confusion. If you find yourself in this type of situation, it is best to end the friendship. It is not worth the stress and drama.

COWORKERS OR BOSSES

Coworkers or employers may also try to gaslight you. If your boss, for example, tells you that your work isn't very good even though you know it is, he might be trying to manipulate you into thinking that you are incompetent so that he can control and intimidate you better. He wants nothing more than for you to question yourself so that he always has the upper hand.

If this happens to you in a professional environment, document everything! Keep track of times when someone tries to make you believe something by making statements like, "You're just saying that because..." or "You think that because..." Write down the words they use along with their tone of voice and body language. Show these notes to other people who have witnessed these conversations and/or email them to yourself, so you have a record. This will help you build a case if things ever go to court or if you need to report this person to HR.

ROMANTIC PARTNERS

Gaslighting is very common in abusive relationships. The abuser will often use gaslighting tactics to make the victim feel like they are crazy and that it is their fault that the abuse is happening. This way, the abuser can maintain control over the victim and keep them from leaving.

If you are in a relationship with someone who is gaslighting you, it is important to get help. It can be very difficult to leave an abusive relationship, but you deserve to be happy and safe. There are many organizations out there that can help you find safe housing and counseling. You are not alone.

In any type of relationship, it is important to trust your own intuition and judgment. If something feels wrong, it probably is. Don't let anyone convince you otherwise. You have the right to be happy and safe in your relationships. You deserve it.

GASLIGHTING FROM STRANGERS

Gaslighting can also happen from strangers. They may make false accusations against you or try to get you in trouble with the authorities. They may even try to get you arrested.

If this happens to you, it is important to stay calm and collected. Don't let them rattle you. Document everything! Get the person's name and contact information, take pictures or video of the encounter, and write down what happened as soon as possible. Contact a lawyer if necessary and file a police report.

No one deserves to be treated this way. You have the right to stand up for yourself and fight back. Don't let anyone victimize you again.

In any type of relationship, it is important to trust your own intuition and judgment. If something feels wrong, it probably is. Don't let anyone convince you otherwise. You have the right to be happy and safe in your relationships. You deserve it.

SUMMARY

Gaslighting is a technique that is often used by narcissists and abusers in order to manipulate their victims. It is a form of psychological abuse that causes the victim to doubt their own judgment and intuition. The abuser will often make false accusations or try to get the victim in trouble with authorities. It can be a very frightening experience and can leave the victim feeling isolated and alone. If this happens to you, it is important to stay calm and collected. Document everything! Get the person's name and contact information, take pictures or video of the encounter, and write down what happened as soon as possible. Contact a lawyer if necessary and file a police report. You have the right to stand up for yourself and fight back.

Free Goodwill

"He who said money can't buy happiness, hasn't given enough away."

UNKNOWN

Helping others (with no expectations of return) leads to greater happiness, a longer life, and greater financial success. I'd like to create the opportunity to deliver this value to you during your reading or listening experience. In order to do this, I have a quick question for you...

Would you help someone you'd never meet even if you might never get credit for it, if it didn't cost you anything?

If so, I have a little 'ask' to make on behalf of someone you do not know. And likely, never will.

They're just like you (or like you were a short time ago): less experienced, in an abusive relationship, full of desire to help the world, seeking information but unsure where to look....this is where you come in.

The only way for us as self-published authors to accomplish our mission of helping people is, first, by reaching them. And as most people do, in fact, judge a book by its cover (and its reviews), a review is one of the most impactful things you can do to help get the word out about this book. If you have found this book valuable thus far, would you please take a brief moment right now and leave an honest review of the book and its contents? It will cost you zero dollars and less than 60 seconds.

Your review will help....

....one more struggling person break free of an abusive relationship.
....one more person live a life they find meaningful.
....one more woman experience a transformation they otherwise would never have encountered.
....one more life change for the better.

To make that happen...all you have to do is....and this takes less than 60 seconds....leave a review.

- If you are on audible - hit the three dots in the top right of your device, click rate & review, then leave a few sentences about the book with a star rating.
- If you are reading on kindle or an e-reader - you can scroll to the bottom of the book, then swipe up and it will automatically prompt a review.

- If for some reason they have changed either functionality - you can go to the book page on amazon (or wherever you purchased this) and leave a review right on the page.

PS - If you feel good about helping a faceless author, you are my kind of people. I'm that much more excited to help you crush it in the coming chapters (you'll love the tactics I'm about to go over).

Thank you from the bottom of my heart. Now back to our regularly scheduled programming.

- Your biggest fan, Georgia

The Impact of Gaslighting

A common question after someone's been subjected to gaslighting is; "Why didn't you just leave?" or "Why did you stay?". It can be hard for outsiders to understand why someone wouldn't just walk away from a difficult situation, especially if they're the victim of repeated manipulation by their significant other. The sad truth is that many gaslighting victims do try to escape but are prevented from doing so by the very nature of the abuse. Gaslighters will often cut off financial resources, threaten their partner with violence and even use children as pawns in order to stop them from leaving. Other tactics include making up false accusations about their target or using friends and colleagues to convey messages which put pressure on them not to leave.

Occasionally gaslighters will resort to extreme measures such as threatening suicide in order to stop their victims from walking out. The truth is that once someone allows themselves to become a victim of gaslighting, it's incredibly difficult for them to escape the abuse and take control over their own lives again. Many victims blame themselves for staying in such toxic relationships and suffer from feelings of worthlessness and self-doubt long after they've escaped.

The impact of gaslighting and psychological manipulation can be deeply traumatizing and seriously damage your confidence, self-esteem, and ability to trust other people in future relationships. Gaslighting has also been known to lead to serious mental health conditions such as depression, eating disorders, anxiety problems, PTSD, or even suicidal thoughts. For this reason, it's essential that anyone who suspects they may be a victim of gaslighting get the help and support they need as soon as possible.

DISBELIEF AND CONFUSION

Disbelief and confusion are common reactions after you've been subjected to gaslighting. If you're finding it hard to trust your own judgment or you feel like you can't even think straight, then it's time to seek professional help. There are many qualified therapists who can assist you in rebuilding your self-esteem and regaining control over your life. The earlier you seek help, the easier it will be to overcome the consequences of gaslighting and begin living your life again.

Recovery from gaslighting is possible but not without significant effort on your part. You need to be strong enough to acknowledge that there's a problem in order to get the right kind of support. Gaslighting abuse must be dealt with before serious mental health problems arise or feelings of low self-worth become permanent.

DEFENSE MECHANISMS

In order to protect themselves from the pain of gaslighting, victims often develop defense mechanisms. These can include denial, avoidance, and rationalization. The aim is to try and make sense of the nonsensical in order to maintain some degree of control over their lives. It's not unusual for gaslighting victims to withdraw from friends and family or even quit their job as they strive to create a bubble around themselves that's free from the gaslighter's influence.

If you're a victim of gaslighting, it's important to understand that your reactions are normal and you're not alone. There are people who can help you rebuild your life after this type of abuse. Seek out counseling or therapy if you need support in dealing with the aftermath of gaslighting.

It's also a good idea to join a support group or online forum for survivors of emotional abuse. The more you understand about gaslighting and the better equipped you are to deal with it, the sooner you'll be able to move on from this abusive relationship and start living your life again.

DEPRESSION

It's not unusual for victims of gaslighting to suffer from depression as a result of the abuse. This is because it affects your self-esteem and ability to trust your own judgment. You may find that you're unable to function effectively or carry out everyday tasks due to feelings of anxiety, stress, and restlessness. Depression can also lead many victims of gaslighting to feel completely overwhelmed by their circumstances and even consider suicide as an option.

ADDICTION

In some cases gaslighting can lead to addiction as a way of coping with the daily abuse they face at the hands of their partner. If this is happening in your life, then you need help immediately before it's too late – especially if you have children involved who are being affected by your choice to stay in the relationship.

The behavior of addiction is often deeply rooted in low self-esteem and distorted thinking patterns. If you're struggling to understand why you feel the need to self-medicate with drugs or alcohol, then it's time to get professional help. It could be that you have underlying issues that are being triggered by your partner's abuse, but until these are dealt with, you'll never find peace or happiness.

Cravings for things like drugs, alcohol, food, or sex are common signs of gaslighting abuse. If this is something you're experiencing on a regular basis, take action now before it becomes too late. Get yourself into treatment so that you can begin rebuilding your life free from fear and anxiety. There are many support groups available to help you understand what's happening to you and ways of coping with the abuse.

OUT OF CONTROL

Many gaslighting victims feel out of control as a result of being forced into submission by their partners. They may experience mood swings, panic attacks, or an inability to concentrate that's directly related to the stress they're under. These are all side effects of emotional abuse, and it can take some time for your brain chemistry to return to its normal balance after this type of trauma. You can help yourself overcome these issues by getting plenty of exercises and engaging in activities that will stimulate positive brain activity, such as painting or writing. If you give yourself something constructive and meaningful to focus on, then it will be easier for you to gradually regain your sense of self.

TIRED ALL THE TIME

Being subjected to emotional abuse through gaslighting can leave you feeling constantly tired, even if you've had plenty of sleep. It's because you're drained by having to deal with this type of daily stress in your life, and in order to cope with it, your body is shutting down in some way. The more often this happens, the weaker your immune system becomes and the less energy you'll have available for yourself. Make sure that you schedule periods when you can relax without distractions or interruptions so that you can revitalize yourself. By doing this regularly, it will become easier for you to overcome any feelings of fatigue or burnout that could otherwise harm your physical wellbeing.

VICTIMIZED

Gaslighting victims often feel like they're living in a nightmare where they can't escape the abuse. This is because the narcissist will quickly tear down your self-esteem until you're convinced that it's all your fault. They will make you believe that you are unworthy of love, respect, or anything else good in life, and as time goes on, this will start to become true.

SHORT-TERM EFFECTS OF GASLIGHTING

The following are all common signs of gaslighting abuse; however, there could be others not listed. With help and support, it's possible to overcome any of the effects below, but if you find yourself unable to cope without professional assistance, then please take action immediately before it becomes too late.

- Panic attacks or anxiety that won't go away
- Mood swings or sudden emotional outbursts for no reason
- Eating disorders such as bulimia, anorexia, or obesity
- Sleeping problems like insomnia or nightmares
- Suicidal thoughts or extreme self-harm (gaslighters will often threaten suicide if their victim tries to leave)

LONG TERM EFFECTS OF GASLIGHTING

It takes a lot of strength and courage to face up to a narcissist and leave an abusive relationship. Many victims find that the long-term effects of gaslighting abuse make it difficult to move on, even after they've escaped. Some of the most common issues include:

- Depression or suicidal thoughts
- PTSD or other forms of trauma
- Difficulty trusting others or forming new relationships
- Low self-esteem or self-hatred
- Drug or alcohol addiction to cope with the pain
- Feeling like you're constantly walking on eggshells around someone who is never satisfied

WHAT SHOULD I DO?

There are many warning signs of gaslighting, and if you see any of them happening in your relationship, please get out now. The longer you stay, the more damage will be done, and it may eventually be too late for you to recover. Don't let yourself become a victim – find the courage to stand up to the abuser and reclaim your life. You deserve so much better.

If you're in a relationship with a narcissist, it's very likely that you're experiencing gaslighting abuse. This is a form of emotional terrorism that can leave you feeling scared, alone, and out of control. If you don't take steps to get help, the effects can be devastating both mentally and physically. Don't wait – here are some things you can do to start rebuilding your life today.

Recognize the signs of gaslighting. If your partner is constantly making you feel like you're crazy or overreacting, then they're probably using this tactic to manipulate you. Other signs include being made to feel guilty for no reason, being isolated from friends and family, and having your reality questioned on a regular basis.

Take action now. Don't spend another day in an abusive relationship. If you're experiencing regular gaslighting, then it's time to take control of your life again and get the abuser out of the picture for good.

WHAT WILL HAPPEN IF I STAY?

If you continue to live with someone who is harming you on a daily basis, there may be long-term emotional effects on your mental wellbeing, including anxiety attacks and paranoia. You could also become depressed about how low you've been brought or find that your relationships with others are becoming increasingly difficult. This type of trauma can affect many aspects of your life, so it's vital that you don't ignore any warning signs but act immediately before the abuse gets even worse. Your physical health could also be affected by a gaslighting narcissist, so try to eat a healthy diet and exercise regularly. When you do this, you'll have more energy available to deal with your emotions and take control of your life again.

Recovering from gaslighting is possible, but it will require patience and time. Don't beat yourself up if things get difficult – many people who've lived through similar situations stay stuck in self-blame for years. It's important that you remember the abuse was never your fault and that no one deserves to make you feel unworthy or inadequate. You deserve to live a happy and fulfilling life, and although it won't happen overnight, it is absolutely possible if you're willing to put in the work.

CHAPTER SUMMARY

In the last chapter, we discussed the short & long-term effects of gaslighting abuse. In this chapter, we're going to look at what factors come into play in a gaslighting relationship and how they can be destructive to both parties. Victims will often experience mental health issues such as anxiety attacks and depression from living with a narcissist that constantly makes them feel crazy or worthless. The abuser may also cause a victim to have a poor diet and lack of exercise, which can lead to physical exhaustion and neglect of their self-care. If you have been in a gaslight in a narcissist's life, there are some steps you can take in order to recover from being so affected by them. They include recognizing the signs, taking action now against the abuser, and seeking professional help. Remember that it takes time and patience to fully recover, but it is absolutely possible with the right tools.

How To Fight Back

Gaslighting is no longer just a relationship problem. This kind of manipulation has gone beyond relationships to politics, even to war. Examine any social or political conflict, and the deeper issue will be revealed as gaslighting of one form or another.

Gaslighting is an insidious form of abuse that is difficult to identify yet even more difficult to break free from because it slowly but surely distorts your sense of reality.

Once you are able to accept that you have been the victim of gaslighting, changing your behavior becomes easier because you know what not to do! You can fight back by using this knowledge about their tactics against them (interestingly enough, this works for both victims and abusers).

If you are the victim of gaslighting in your relationship, you must change your behavior. If you want to stop being the victim of gaslighting, you must first be aware that it is happening. Second, recognize what is happening while it is happening, third understand where it came from, fourth see how it works, and lastly, break free by refusing to engage with the abuser any longer. You must make a commitment to yourself that no matter what reaction they elicit out of you by their abuse, this time around, the reaction will not be played out. By doing this, you are taking away all control that they have over what happens next in the interaction, which always follows predictable patterns based on old scripts. Remember, these are psychological games that the abuser plays in order to get a reaction.

So how do you overcome this insidious trick?

STAND UP FOR YOURSELF

If you can manage to find your voice and speak up for yourself and what you believe in, then you have taken back some of that power. This will undoubtedly make them angry, but do not engage with them any further. It is important to remember that anger is just another tool that the abuser uses to keep you under their thumb. Responding in anger will only give them more ammunition to use against you in the future.

It takes time and practice, but eventually, you will be able to see through their games and react accordingly. Keep in mind, though, that it is very likely that the abuser will not change, and you must learn to accept them for who they are and what they did to you while at the same time knowing that you did nothing wrong.

Fear is an important part of any relationship; we all feel it from time to time, but if we allow it to take over our lives, then we lose sight of reality. It can be difficult to understand why someone would try so hard to control us like this, but the reasons stem back from childhood, where most abusers experienced some form of abuse themselves that made them into the person they are today. If your abuser was never validated as a child or if their own experience with abuse was more traumatic than normal (i.e., emotional neglect), then understanding their behavior becomes easier because then their behavior is no longer personal. The abuser isn't doing this to hurt you, but they are hurting nonetheless, and their way of coping with that abuse is to inflict it onto other people.

Once you understand the tactics at play, you will never again be an easy victim because your eyes have been opened to them. You will begin to be aware of the warning signs before any real damage occurs, and other forms of emotional abuse will not affect you as easily. It takes practice to break free from these control issues, but it is possible if you start by first finding yourself again and then move on towards building a healthy relationship with yourself and someone else in the future.

BALANCE YOUR EMOTIONAL STATE

A healthy relationship should not feel like you are constantly walking on eggshells. You should feel safe to be yourself, quirks and all. If something feels off, then it probably is, and it's time to reassess the situation. Trust your gut instinct; it has saved you from a lot of heartache in the past.

Creating this balance in your life is key to recovering from any type of abusive relationship because it helps to build self-confidence and a sense of trust that was likely damaged during the gaslighting experience. It is also important to find people who will support you through this process, people who will not judge you but rather offer a listening ear and advice when needed. People can be hard to find, but they are out there.

The abuser will never change. This is something that you must come to terms with if you want to move on from the relationship. It is not your fault, and you did nothing wrong. The abuser is responsible for their own actions, no matter how much they try to make you think otherwise.

Building a healthy relationship takes time, effort, and a lot of work, but it is worth it in the end. Remember that you are not alone in this, and there are people who care about you and want to see you happy and thriving. Take the first step towards recovery by seeking help either from a friend, family member, or therapist. It's time to break free from the chains of gaslighting and build a life you love.

IN CASE YOU CAN'T LEAVE.

If you can't leave the relationship, then there are still things you can do to protect yourself. First and foremost, get rid of anything that could be used as a weapon against you (including knives, firearms, and any type of drug) and keep them in a safe place where the abuser cannot access them. If possible, create a safety plan that can be put into effect if you find yourself in a situation where you could be seriously injured. This includes having an 'escape' bag packed with your important documents and some form of identification, as well as extra money, clothes, etc.

Additionally, it's best to have a code phrase or signal that lets other people know that something is happening so they can call for help. It should look like a normal conversation but include a hidden message about what is going on inside the home - it doesn't matter what type of language you use as long as those who are able to help understand exactly what is happening. Something subtle like "Did you see the weather outside today?" might mean "I need support right now." The idea behind this tactic is to give others a head's up while also distracting the abuser long enough for you to make your escape or get help.

It might seem impossible right now, but this too shall pass. It may take weeks, months, or even years (and there are no guarantees), but eventually, the time will come when he leaves. When that happens, remember that it's okay to take care of yourself and bask in all of the attention you've been missing out on; don't let anybody make you feel guilty about finally taking some "me" time!

FACING YOUR GASLIGHTER

This is the time to face your abuser and let them know how you feel about their behavior. It might not always go as planned, but it's important that you stand up for yourself and set some boundaries.

That being said, there are no hard and fast rules for this conversation. Each situation is different and will require a unique approach depending on your past experiences with the person in question. If you think therapy might be the right option for you, here are some tips for how to make the most out of these sessions:

First of all, try to avoid talking about the gaslighting experience during therapy (or at least not at first). Instead, focus on what led up to it and why the relationship became abusive in the first place; this will help you get a better understanding of the abuser's behavior and why it's so difficult to break free.

Secondly, be prepared for the abuser to deny everything. They will probably try to turn the blame on you, making you out to be the bad guy or girl in the situation. It's important to stay strong and not give in; eventually, they will have to face up to their own actions.

Therapy can also be a good opportunity to learn more about yourself. What were the weaknesses that the abuser exploited? What type of personality do you have that might have made you vulnerable in the first place? Understanding these things can help make sure you don't get into another abusive relationship in the future.

It's also important to build a support system outside of therapy. This might include friends, family members, or even a support group specifically for people who have been through gaslighting experiences. These people can offer emotional support and practical advice when you need it most.

HOW TO LEAVE AN ABUSIVE RELATIONSHIP

Leaving an abusive relationship can be one of the most difficult things you'll ever do, but it's not impossible. Here are a few tips to help make the process a little bit easier:

First, try to make a safety plan. This should include gathering important documents like your birth certificate, social security card, and driver's license; having some cash on hand in case you need to leave quickly; and finding a safe place to stay (either with friends or family members, if possible). If you have any pets, you'll also need to make arrangements for them as well.

Secondly, don't try to do it alone. Talk to your friends and family members about what's going on; they may want to help you, and they might be able to make it easier once the time comes. You can also talk to a lawyer about your legal rights and how you can keep yourself safe in the future.

Lastly, realize that this isn't your fault. It takes a lot of courage to leave an abusive relationship, but it's something that millions of people have done before you. In fact, most survivors reported having a better quality of life after leaving their abuser behind.

THE GASLIGHTING GUIDE FOR WOMEN:

TIPS FOR DEALING WITH GASLIGHTERS

- Remember that the gaslighter is the one who is responsible for their own actions. Don't take the blame for what's happening in the relationship.
- Don't try to change or fix the gaslighter; this is impossible and will only lead to frustration on your part.
- Set boundaries and stick to them. If the gaslighter crosses a boundary, let them know that this behavior is not acceptable and that you will not tolerate it.
- Seek therapy if you feel like you can't leave the relationship on your own. There are many resources available for people who find themselves in this type of situation, and a therapist or counselor can help you work through it and make sure you're safe.

CONCLUSION

As we mentioned earlier, there is no one-size-fits-all approach to gaslighting. Each victim reacts differently, and since we all have unique relationships with our abusers, we must take every experience as an individual problem that requires an individual solution. No matter what kind of relationship you have with your abuser, however, the important thing is that you don't let them control your life anymore. You're stronger than they think! Gaslighters love to play games; now it's time for us to see how good they are at losing.

CHAPTER SUMMARY

Gaslighting is a form of manipulation that is used to make the victim doubt their own reality. It can be very difficult to leave an abusive relationship, but there are steps that can be taken to make the process a little bit easier. Survivors of gaslighting often find themselves in better-quality relationships after leaving their abuser behind.

Recovering From Abuse And Narcissism

Abuse in any form takes a long time to heal from. You cannot go through an abusive event and be the same after it as when you were before. Narcissistic abuse is particularly difficult because not only have you been abused by someone who doesn't truly care about you, but there is also a whole system of supporters around the narcissist that constantly gaslight you to convince you that your reality isn't real. To make things even more complicated, this system will often include other narcissists or what I call flying monkeys (people that enable the narcissist's behavior). They take their cues from the narcissist and help keep their smear campaign going without questioning anything. Often times they're family members and friends, and they make it their mission to make you feel as awful as possible.

It is incredibly difficult to remove those people from your life, but you have to do what you can. It's a sad fact of abusive relationships, but they're usually filled with enablers and flying monkeys that want the narcissist happy at any cost -- even if that means making you feel horrible. I've been involved in plenty of cases where the family has turned against the victim for no good reason. They'll often say things like the narcissist would never lie, or they always speak highly of them, so clearly they couldn't be lying about all these terrible things... The truth is far more sinister than that because, again, abusers are master manipulators who know exactly how to get what they want.

There is a light at the end of the tunnel, though. You will eventually get to a place where you can start to heal. It's not going to be easy, and it's going to take time, but you will get there. You have to remember that you are worth it and that you deserve to be happy in life. Surround yourself with positive people that make you feel good about yourself, and don't be afraid to cut out anyone that makes you feel bad. Narcissists feed off of your pain, so don't give them the satisfaction. Move on with your life and be happy!

THE GASLIGHTING GUIDE FOR WOMEN:

VICTIM OR VICTORIOUS?

The choice is always yours. You can choose to be a victim, or you can choose to be victorious. I know it's not easy, and the road ahead may seem daunting, but you can do it. You have to want it for yourself, and you have to be willing to fight for it. It won't be easy, but it will be worth it in the end. Remember, you are not alone. There are others out there that have gone through similar things, and they understand what you're going through. Lean on them for support; they will help you get through this.

EDUCATE YOURSELF

One of the most important things you can do is educate yourself about narcissism and narcissistic abuse. This will help you understand what you're dealing with, and it will give you the tools you need to break free from the manipulations. There are plenty of resources out there, both online and in print. Don't be afraid to ask for help, either. There are many people out there that want to help victims of narcissistic abuse.

LOVE YOURSELF

Above all else, you have to learn to love yourself. Yes, I know this sounds weird in a book about narcissistic abuse but hear me out for a minute. You cannot love what you do not accept, and you cannot accept what you don't know. It's one of the universal truths of life.

For many years I didn't truly believe in myself because of the horrible things my ex-boyfriend said about me whenever she was angry with me. She would make fun of everything that I loved and belittle me over everything that I did wrong. Eventually, it started to sink in even though it wasn't true, which is why she continued with the treatment day after day -- because it worked! Even though I knew most of what she said wasn't true, I still internalized it to some extent, and it stopped me from doing many things that I wanted to do.

It wasn't until after I left her that I really started to love myself for who I was. I accepted the things that she said about me as lies, and I moved on. It was hard, but it was worth it in the end. Now, I have a much better relationship with myself, and I know that I'm worth fighting for.

The same thing can happen to you if you allow it. Don't let the narcissist win! You have to learn to love yourself first and foremost so that they no longer have any power over you.

LET GO OF CLOSURE

This is a tough one because we all want closure. We want to be able to put the past behind us and move on with our lives, but that's not always possible, especially when it comes to narcissistic abuse. The thing you have to remember is that closure is ideal; it doesn't exist in reality.

What we often refer to as closure is actually just a band-aid for the soul. It's something that we think will make us feel better, but it doesn't. In fact, it usually has the opposite effect because it keeps us stuck in the past. We can't heal if we're constantly going over what happened and trying to make sense of it.

The best way to move on is to let go of closure and simply let things happen as they will. You can't force someone to tell you how they feel or what went wrong. They either want to tell you, or they don't, plain and simple. If you keep pressuring them for an answer, then it won't be a good one because it wasn't given freely.

If that's the case, then there is no need to know what happened because whatever it was that happened doesn't really matter anyway except in your mind. So save yourself some heartache and release the idea of closure right now before it ruins your life like it ruined mine!

FORGET SHAME, GUILT, AND RESPONSIBILITY

You have to stop feeling shame, guilt, and responsibility for what happened. Even if you did do something wrong, it doesn't give anyone the right to treat you in a degrading manner, especially someone who claims to love you.

I remember when my ex-boyfriend started cheating on me, I felt an immense amount of shame because I believed that I was not worthy of being loved by him or anyone else for that matter. It was the worst type of shame because it struck at my very core.

The thing is, though, there is nothing shameful about loving someone more than they love you back or making mistakes in a relationship! We all make them, but that's not where our focus needs to be. Take responsibility for your part in the relationship, and then forgive yourself. It's okay to make mistakes; we all do!

Once you accept your mistakes for what they were and let go of the shame and guilt, you can finally start to heal.

MEDITATE AND SPEND TIME ALONE...SERIOUSLY!

This is one of the most important things that I did when I was getting over my narcissistic abuse. I started meditating daily, which helped me to see myself in a completely different light. Suddenly everything changed! All of my fears went away, all of my addictions disappeared, and I actually felt empowered by my experiences rather than traumatized by them.

Here's why: Meditation helps us to understand ourselves on a deeper level. It allows us to see the truth, even if it's something that we don't want to see. It gives us the ability to accept things for what they are instead of what we want them to be. This is so important when it comes to narcissistic abuse because we often have a skewed view of reality.

The same thing goes for spending time alone. This is another great way to get to know yourself on a deeper level and to start trusting your intuition again. One of the biggest problems with narcissistic abuse is that we lose trust in ourselves and our intuition. We become so used to following the narcissist's lead that we forget how to trust our own instincts.

Start by taking time for yourself, maybe an hour or two each day. Just relax and allow yourself to be at peace. Don't think about the past or the future; just focus on the present moment. This is where your power lies!

REBUILD YOURSELF

This is probably the most important step of all! You have to rebuild yourself into the person that you want to be, not the person that the narcissist wants you to be. This means that you need to start doing things that make you happy and make you feel good about yourself.

Maybe this means starting a new hobby, going for walks in nature, reading books, or spending time with loved ones. Whatever it is, just do it! The more you do things that make you happy and feel good about yourself, the stronger you will become.

RECONNECT WITH YOUR HIGHER SELF

This is another important step in rebuilding yourself. Once you have reconnected with your Higher Self, you will start to receive guidance and support from the universe. You will also start to see the truth more clearly and be able to discern between what is healthy for you and what is not.

The most important thing is to stay positive and have faith that things will get better!

THE ART OF VOLUNTEERING

I personally believe that there is no better way to heal than by helping others. When we help other people, we not only help ourselves but the world as a whole.

Simply by doing something nice for someone else on a daily basis, you will start to feel much happier about yourself and about your future. This will also help to build your self-esteem and give you the confidence that you need to succeed.

There are so many wonderful causes out there that deserve our support! Volunteering is a great way to connect with others and to give back. Make a difference in the world today by helping those who are less fortunate than yourself; it's a win-win situation for everyone!

GIVE YOURSELF CREDIT...FOR EVERYTHING THAT YOU DO WELL!

It may seem silly, but this is another important step towards healing from narcissistic abuse. It can be very hard for us survivors to accept praise or credit for things that we think of as "easy" or not as important as someone else's achievement.

The truth is, though, everything that you do matters. Everything that you do is important; everything that you accomplish should be applauded! Don't underestimate your value or worth; every little thing that you do has an impact on the world around us.

Put yourself first for once and start accepting credit for all of the wonderful things that you have done. This will help to boost your self-esteem and to feel good about yourself again!

LISTEN TO YOUR BODY'S WISDOM

Our bodies are incredible beings that are always trying to keep us safe. We just need to listen to them more often in order to stay safe and secure.

If we pay attention, we can learn a great deal from our bodies, including how we really feel about someone or something, as well as our intuition about a particular situation.

Start by noticing how your body feels when you are around the narcissist. Do you feel tense or anxious? Does your stomach churn, or do you feel like you can't breathe? These are all signs that something is wrong and that you need to get away from the narcissist as soon as possible!

Your intuition will also come in handy when it comes to making decisions about relationships. If something doesn't feel right, then chances are it's not right for you! Trust your intuition; it will never steer you wrong!

GRIEVE THE LOSSES

This is another very important step in the healing process. We need to grieve all of the losses that we have suffered as a result of the narcissist's abuse. This includes the loss of our self-esteem, our trust, our innocence, and our sense of security.

It's also important to grieve the loss of the relationship itself. The relationship was not healthy for us, and it likely caused us a great deal of pain. It's natural to feel sad and lonely after a break-up, but try to remember that the relationship was not good for you.

ALLOW YOURSELF TO FEEL THE EMOTIONS FULLY

Many survivors find themselves trying to suppress their emotions, or they try to "fix" them as quickly as possible. It's important to allow yourself to feel all of the emotions that you are feeling, even if they are very difficult or painful.

Unfortunately, this will not be an easy process, but it is extremely important in order for us to heal fully and properly. If we do not take the time to sit with our emotions, then we may end up bottling them up inside, which can lead to a whole host of other issues down the road.

ACCEPT WHAT HAPPENED AND WHO YOU ARE TODAY!

In many ways accepting what happened and who you are today is one of the most challenging steps on this list. In order to truly accept what happened, we need to stand in the truth about what the narcissist did to us and how they made us feel.

And, we need to accept who we are today; this means accepting all of our strengths and weaknesses as well as accepting our limitations! When we truly do this, then we can stop putting ourselves down or feeling like less than because of the narcissistic abuse that has happened to us. We deserve unconditional self-compassion and self-love just as much as anyone else!

CREATE NEW RELATIONSHIPS

It's very important that we start to create new relationships for ourselves. It can be difficult at first, but it is always better than trying to hang on to an old and broken relationship!

Try not to compare your new partner or potential partner in any way with the narcissist because chances are they will never live up to their expectations anyways. Remember, you deserve unconditional love and acceptance just as much as anyone else does.

GIVE IT TIME

This step is so very important and so very crucial. We need to give the process of healing time. Otherwise, we may end up feeling frustrated or stuck.

The truth is that it took a very long time for the narcissist to break down your self-esteem and confidence as well as pushing you into believing that you are worthless or stupid. It will take some work on your part, but eventually, you will relearn how to love yourself again!

YOU ARE NOT ALONE

I want to end this by saying again that you are not alone. There are others out there that have gone through similar things, and they understand what you're going through. Lean on them for support; they will help you get through this. Together we can raise awareness about narcissistic abuse and help others know they are not alone.

CHAPTER SUMMARY

Gaslighting is a form of emotional abuse that can be very difficult to recognize. Narcissists are experts at manipulating and controlling their victims, often using gaslighting tactics to break down their self-esteem and confidence. It is important to be aware of the signs of gaslighting in order to protect yourself from this type of abuse. There are many steps involved in healing from narcissistic abuse, but it is possible to recover and rebuild your life. You are not alone in this process.

Final Words

If you've been gaslit, manipulated, or abused by a narcissistic person in your life, I hope this book has given you hope. It has also offered some practical advice on how to protect yourself from this type of abuse. With any luck, you now feel that you have the tools to help you recognize these types of people before they become too involved in your life.

In many ways, the experiences you have been through with a narcissistic person in your life will always be a part of who you are. By recognizing this and using this information to try and help yourself grow stronger, I hope that you can use these memories as a source of strength going forward into the future.

FINAL WORDS

If there is one thing I want you to remember from reading this book, it's how valuable and unique each human being on the planet really is. Despite all their flaws and shortcomings, we can't forget that narcissists only exist because they rely on the vulnerabilities of others to exist. So, don't forget your own power and potential – you are the only one who can change your life for the better!

So, if you're feeling like it's time for a change in your life, I encourage you to go out there and make it happen. The future is always uncertain, but that doesn't mean we can't control how we react to the challenges that come our way. Stay strong and remember, you are not alone.

Thank you for reading! If you found this book helpful and would like to see more content like this, please consider leaving a review on Amazon.

Acknowledgments

This book is a culmination of over ten years of research and study on the topic of gaslighting. In this acknowledgment section, I would like to thank all those that have helped me with my personal relationships, as well as for all their work that went into researching and writing this book.

First off, I would like to thank my friends and family who have put up with me over the years, knowing that I was writing this book. The conversations we've had about gaslighting have helped all of us be able to communicate better. To say thanks for putting up with me, I will not disclose any embarrassing stories or events. These are our stories, and you can't have them!

Second, thanks go out to my Mom, who started me off on the road of self-help many years ago by buying me Stephen Covey's "Seven Habits Of Highly Effective People." It was because of her that I got stressed enough at one point in my life (after reading it) that caused me to go back into therapy. I needed help learning how to deal with my emotions.

To my friends who helped review this book for accuracy, thank you! It was your willingness to read early drafts that made it easier for me to make the necessary changes. I have found that you learn the most from your own experiences, but having an outside opinion can give you a fresh perspective. I would like to thank them for their honesty.

My editor, Charisse Kiino, has been working on my writing for the last decade and always manages to make it feel like we are talking in person while editing the book. Thank you very much for sharing this journey with me!

The staff at Create Space/Amazon KDP ... a big THANK YOU for taking care of all the details so that the author doesn't have to worry about anything except writing! You made publishing this book incredibly easy!

To YOU . . . if, after reading this book, you decide that gaslighting is going on in your life, I hope that you will find the courage to take back your power and live a healthier life.

About the Author

Georgia Ray is an author and mom of 3 who writes about relationships, empowering women, and overcoming obstacles in life. After spending years in the corporate world, she decided to pursue her passion for writing and now writes full-time, having had her work has been featured on numerous websites and publications. She is a strong believer in the power of writing to change lives, and hopes to see it continue to grow in the future.

Georgia attended Emerson College in Boston, where she earned her degree in Creative Writing. She lives with her family of five (including their dog, Biscuit) on the West Coast. Her hobbies include sleeping late and drinking coffee at all hours of the day.

Georgia's motto is: *"no woman should suffer alone".*

References

1. "APA Dictionary of Psychology". *APA.org*. American Psychological Association. Retrieved 7 July 2021.
2. "Definition of gaslight (Entry 2 of 2)". Merriam Webster.
3. DiGiulio, Sarah. "What is gaslighting? And how do you know if it's happening to you?". *nbcnews.com*. NBC News.com. Retrieved 13 July 2018.
4. "Gaslight". *oed.com*. Oxford English Dictionary. Retrieved 25 October 2021. Etymology: the title of George Cukor's 1944 film Gaslight
5. Yagoda, Ben (12 January 2017). "How Old Is 'Gaslighting'?". *The Chronicle of Higher Education*. Retrieved 2 June 2017.

REFERENCES

6. Metcalf, Allan. "2016 Word of the Year" (PDF). American Dialect Society. Retrieved 6 January 2017. most useful word of the year
7. "Word of the Year 2018: Shortlist". Oxford University Press. Retrieved 15 November 2018.
8. Holland, Brenna. "For Those Who Experience Gaslighting, the Widespread Misuse of the Word Is Damaging". *wellandgood.com*. Well + Good. Retrieved 2 September 2021.
9. Gass PhD, Gertrude Zemon; Nichols EdD, William C. (18 March 1988). "Gaslighting: A marital syndrome". *Contemp Family Therapy*. 8: 3–16. doi:10.1007/BF00922429. S2CID 145019324.
10. Dorpat, Theodore L. (1996). *Gaslighting, the Double Whammy, Interrogation, and Other Methods of Covert Control in Psychotherapy and Psychoanalysis*. Northvale, NJ: Jason Aronson. ISBN 978-1-56821-828-1. OCLC 34548677. Retrieved 24 April 2021.
11. Lund, C.A.; Gardiner, A.Q. (1977). "The Gaslight Phenomenon: An Institutional Variant". *British Journal of Psychiatry*. 131 (5): 533–34. doi:10.1192/bjp.131.5.533. PMID 588872.
12. Barlow, D. H. (January 2010). "Special section on negative effects from psychological

treatments". *American Psychologist.* 65 (1): 13–49. doi:10.1037/a0015643. PMID 20063906.
13. Basseches, Michael (April 1997). "A developmental perspective on psychotherapy process, psychotherapists' expertise, and 'meaning-making conflict' within therapeutic relationships: part II". *Journal of Adult Development.* 4 (2): 85–106. doi:10.1007/BF02510083. S2CID 143991100. Basseches coined the term "theoretical abuse" as a parallel to "sexual abuse" in psychotherapy.
14. Abramson, Kate (2014). "Turning up the Lights on Gaslighting". *Philosophical Perspectives.* 28 (1): 1–30. doi:10.1111/phpe.12046. ISSN 1520-8583.
15. Portnow, Kathryn E. (1996). *Dialogues of doubt: the psychology of self-doubt and emotional gaslighting in adult women and men* (EdD). Cambridge, MA: Harvard Graduate School of Education. OCLC 36674740. ProQuest 619244657.
16. Sarkis, Stephanie (2018). *Gaslighting: Recognize Manipulative and Emotionally Abusive People – and Break Free.* Da Capo Press. ISBN 978-0738284668. OCLC 1023486127.
17. Stern PhD, Robin (19 December 2018). "I've counseled hundreds of victims of gaslighting.

REFERENCES

Here's how to spot if you're being gaslighted. Gaslighting, explained". *vox.com/*. Vox. Retrieved 3 January 2019.

18. Jacobson, Neil S.; Gottman, John M. (1998). *When Men Batter Women: New Insights into Ending Abusive Relationships*. Simon and Schuster. pp. 129–132. ISBN 978-0-684-81447-6. Retrieved 6 January 2014.

19. Stout, Martha (14 March 2006). *The Sociopath Next Door*. Random House Digital. pp. 94–95. ISBN 978-0-7679-1582-3. Retrieved 6 January 2014.

20. Nelson, Hilde L. (March 2001). *Damaged identities, narrative repair*. Cornell University Press. pp. 31–32. ISBN 978-0-8014-8740-8. Retrieved 6 January 2014.

21. Simon, George (8 November 2011). "Gaslighting as a Manipulation Tactic: What It Is, Who Does It, And Why". *CounsellingResource.com: Psychology, Therapy & Mental Health Resources*. Retrieved 13 April 2018.

22. Welch, Bryant (2008). *State of Confusion: Political Manipulation and the Assault on the American Mind*. New York: Thomas Dunne Books, St. Martin's Press. ISBN 978-0312373061. OCLC 181601311. gaslighting.

REFERENCES

23. Ghitis, Frida. "Donald Trump is 'gaslighting' all of us". CNN. Retrieved 16 February 2017.
24. Paolucci, Paul B. (2019). *Acquiring Modernity: An Investigation into the Rise, Structure, and Future of the Modern World*. Brill. ISBN 978-90-04-39395-0.
25. Dowd, Maureen (26 November 1995). "Opinion | Liberties; The Gaslight Strategy". *The New York Times*. Retrieved 5 November 2021.
26. Gibson, Caitlin (27 January 2017). "What we talk about when we talk about Donald Trump and 'gaslighting'". *The Washington Post*. ISSN 0190-8286.
27. Dominus, Susan (27 September 2016). "The Reverse-Gaslighting of Donald Trump". *The New York Times Magazine*. Retrieved 23 January 2017.
28. Duca, Lauren (10 December 2016). "Donald Trump Is Gaslighting America". *Teen Vogue*. Retrieved 23 January 2017.
29. Fox, Maggie (25 January 2017). "Some Experts Say Trump Team's Falsehoods Are Classic 'Gaslighting'". *NBC News*. Retrieved 8 March 2017.
30. From 'alternative facts' to rewriting history in Trump's White House, BBC, Jon Sopel, 26 July 2018

REFERENCES

31. Carol Anne Constabile-Heming & Valentina Glajar & Alison Lewis (2021). "Citizen informants, glitches in the system, and the limits of collaboration: Eastern experiences in the cold war era". In Andreas Marklund & Laura Skouvig (ed.). *Histories of Surveillance from Antiquity to the Digital Era: The Eyes and Ears of Power*. Routledge.
32. Ellen, Barbara. "In accusing all creeps of gaslighting, we dishonour the real victims". *theguardian.com*. The Guardian. Retrieved 6 July 2019.
33. "'Days of Our Lives': Will Gabi Hernandez Face Any Consequences for Her Actions?". 17 November 2018.
34. Yahr, Emily (10 October 2016). "'The Girl on the Train': Let's discuss that twisted ending". *The Washington Post*. ISSN 0190-8286. Retrieved 13 April 2018.
35. BBC. "Changing the world's longest running drama: How The Archers is continuing despite the coronavirus pandemic". *bbc.co.uk*. BBC. Retrieved 5 December 2021.
36. Haider, Arwa. "A cultural history of gaslighting". *bbc.com*. BBC. Retrieved 22 November 2019.
37. Watts, Jay (5 April 2016). "The Archers domestic abuse is classic 'gaslighting' – very real, little

understood". *The Guardian*. Retrieved 22 April 2017.
38. Sakamoto, John. "The Steely Dan Q&A". *steelydanreader.com*. The Steely Dan Reader. Retrieved 28 February 2015. Sakamoto: What does the title of the first track, "Gaslighting Abbie," mean? Fagen: ..the term "to gaslight" comes from the film Gaslight... So it's really a certain kind of mind fucking, or messing with somebody's head by... Becker: That's sort of the rich old tradition of gaslighting which we were invoking.

www.ingramcontent.com/pod-product-compliance
Lightning Source LLC
Chambersburg PA
CBHW021429070526
44577CB00001B/123